# OUR STORY
## How we became a family

DONOR CONCEPTION NETWORK

Text by Nina Barnsley and Stephanie Clarkson
Illustrations by Gabi Froden
Editing and Project Management by Stephanie Clarkson
Designed by Andy Archer
Produced by the 38a The Shop www.38atheshop.com
Published by the Donor Conception Network

©2018 Donor Conception Network

All rights reserved. No part of this publication may be reproduced, stored in a retrieval system or transmitted by any means, electronic, mechanical, photocopying or otherwise, without the prior permission in writing of the publisher.

Acknowledgements

The Donor Conception Network would like to thank the April Trust for their support in the production of these new **Our Story** books. We would also like to acknowledge Angela Mays and Jane Offord who wrote the inspirational **My Story** for sperm donation families in 1991 which was so important in helping families to be open with their children.

ISBN: 978-1-910222-64-5

Our Story 008 HCED2

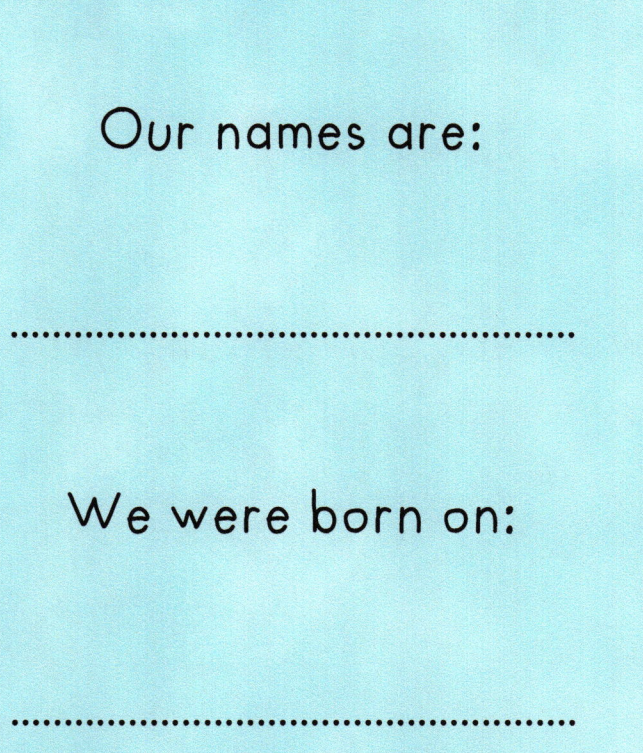

Our names are:

..............................................................

We were born on:

..............................................................

This is the story of our family.

Before we were born, Mummy and Daddy loved each other very much.

One day, they decided they wanted
a baby to love and look after.

Mummy and Daddy tried to have a baby and they were sad when it didn't happen.

What could they do? Who could help?

They decided to go to see the doctor.

To make a baby you need a seed from a man, an egg from a woman and a nice warm tummy to grow the baby in.

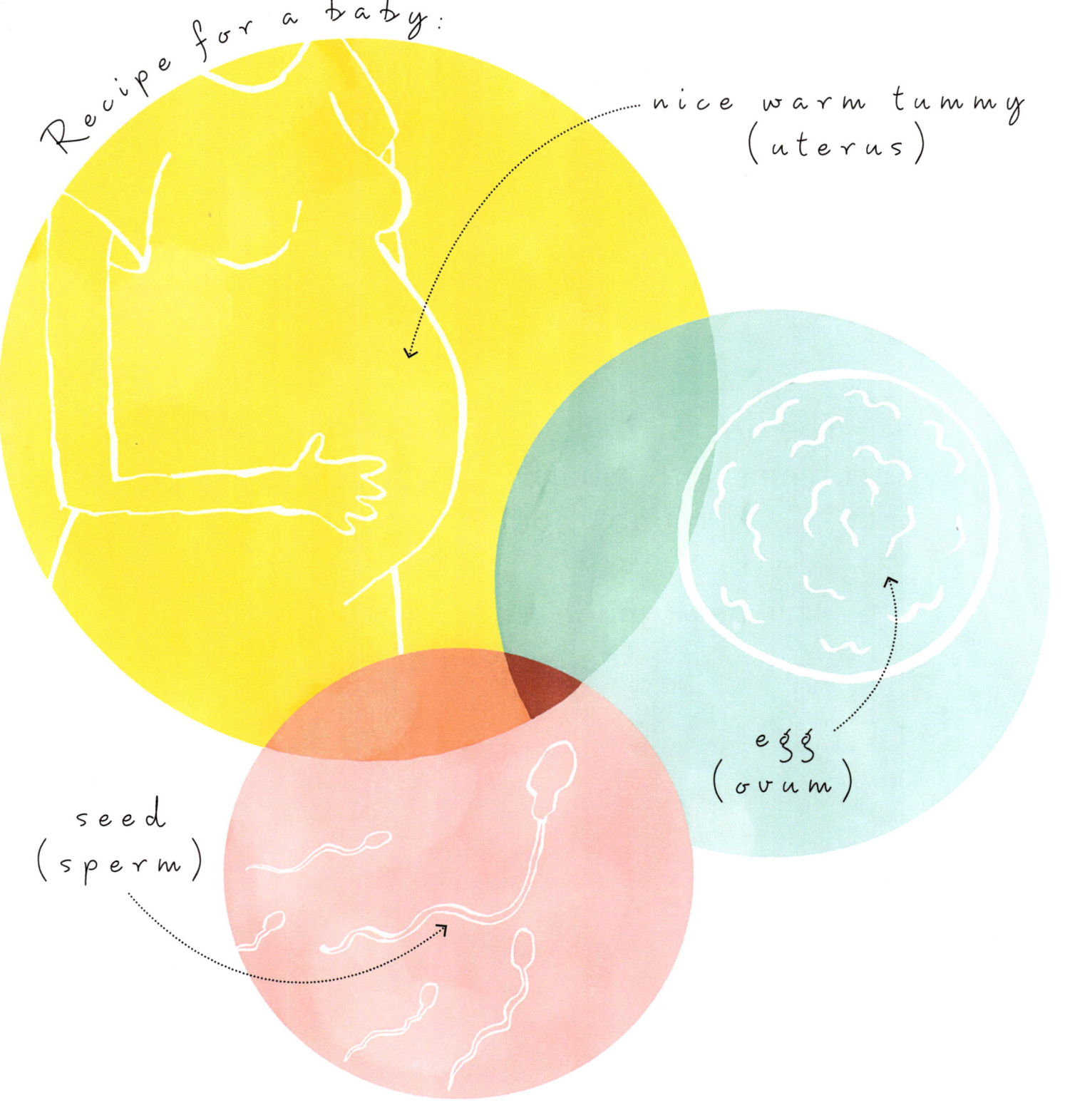

The doctor explained that there were problems with Mummy's eggs, which meant a baby couldn't grow.

This news made Mummy and Daddy feel very sad.

Then the doctor told them there
was still a way for them to have a baby,
but they would need some extra help.

There are women who give some of their eggs to help other people make a baby. They are called donors.

Lots of different people choose to be donors because they want to do something kind and help people like Mummy and Daddy to have children.

Mummy and Daddy were really happy to hear that there was a way they could have a baby to love.

They decided to give it a try.

When the time was right,
they went to the clinic. The doctor
put Daddy's seeds together with the
donor's eggs in Mummy's tummy.

Then they had to wait to see
if a baby would grow...

And guess what!

Two babies grew.

How amazing is that?

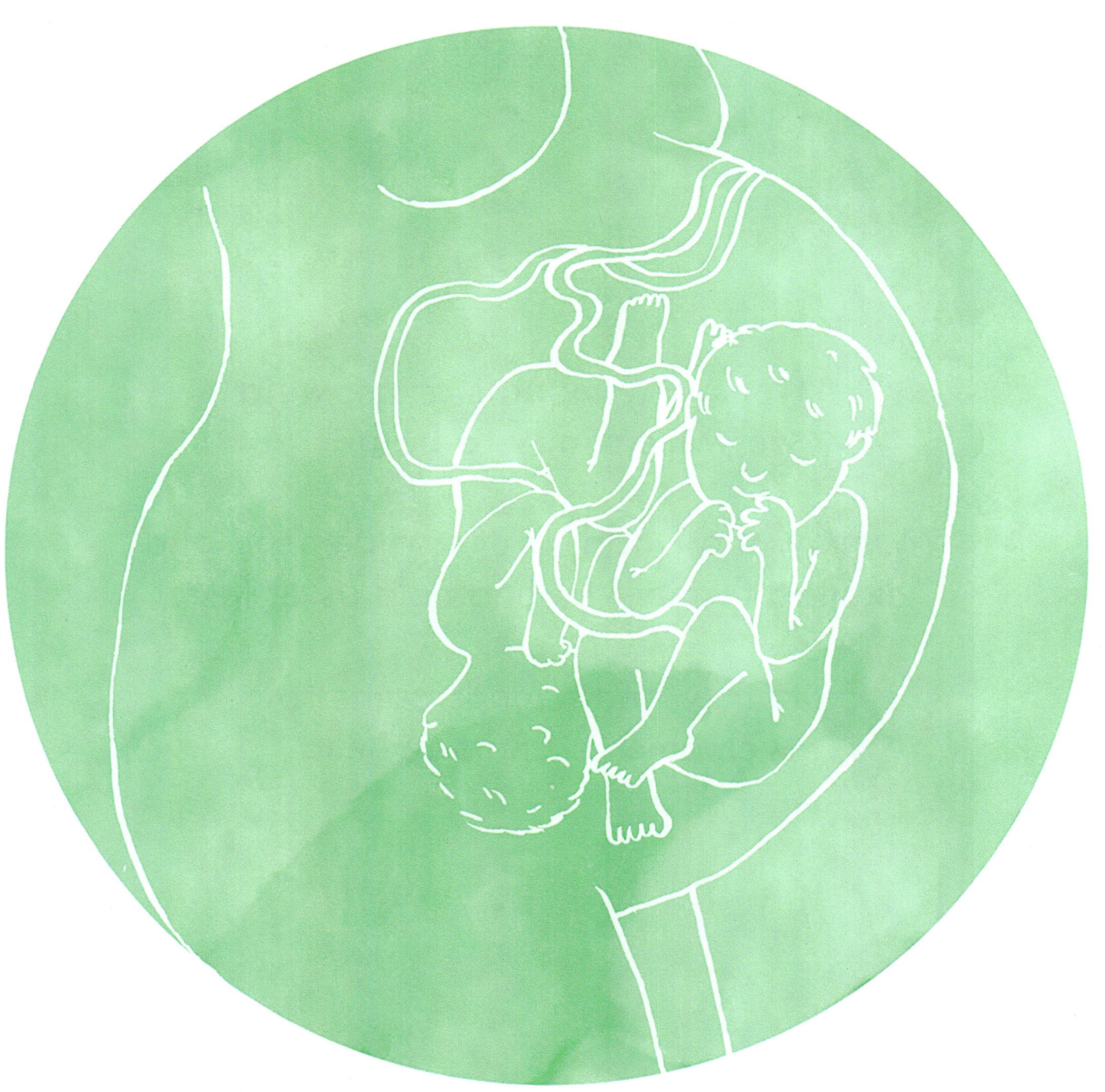

After many months of growing
we were ready to be born.

Mummy and Daddy were so pleased and
excited to meet us and hold us at last.

Family and friends came to
welcome us and say hello.

There are many different ways that families are made and they come in all shapes and sizes.

This is how we began and how
our family was made.

It is our story.

Here is a picture of us together.

Mummy and Daddy are very proud
of our family and they are so grateful
to everyone who helped make us.

www.ingramcontent.com/pod-product-compliance
Lightning Source LLC
Chambersburg PA
CBHW061401090426
42743CB00002B/103